I0103965

Limits of Liability and Disclaimer of Warranty
The author and publisher shall not be liable for your misuse of this material. This book is strictly for informational purposes. The purpose of this book is to educate and entertain. The author and publisher do not guarantee anyone following these techniques, suggestions, tips, ideas, or strategies will become successful. The author and publisher shall have neither liability nor responsibility to anyone with respect to any loss or damage caused, or alleged to be caused, directly or indirectly by the information contained in this book. Views expressed in this publication do not necessarily reflect the views of the publisher.

Printed in the United States of America
ISBN: 979-8-218-25461-2

UNKNOWN LABELS

KNOW ME BEFORE YOU LABEL ME

Dr. Perry D. Mills, Sr.

This book is dedicated to all the students I served as principal from 2009–2017 at Blythewood Academy. The relationships we built led me to truly see how so many were misunderstood.

I also dedicate this book to the teachers and staff who not only supported me in this role but also embraced my passion and love for the students we served to create a culture of caring.

CONTENTS

Introduction

"Labels are for filing. Labels are for clothing. Labels are not for people."
— Martina Navratilova —

For years, I contemplated and dreamed about writing a book based on my concern that there was a stereotype around the students considered "at risk." When I first became a teacher, I taught in an alternative school for discipline and, after teaching in this school for three years, I accelerated my trajectory to become the principal of a different alternative school for discipline two years later and served in that capacity for an additional eight years.

In those eight years, it weighed heavy on my heart that the title "at risk" that was associated with our students was damaging. Many of the students I served in those years were African American and predominantly male. When we start to put a label on our students, unfortunately, some turn out to be what they are called. I believe there is power in words, so it is my opinion that we must be careful about the words we use and how we relate those words to our students.

During the time I served as principal, I decided to return to the classroom as a student myself to earn my doctorate degree. When I began that program, I knew that I wanted to research alternative schools, with a heavy emphasis on the disproportionate number of students of color therein. The study would go on to be one of a comparison between South Carolina and North Carolina students placed in alternative schools for discipline. During my dissertation and research, I found that more than 85% of students in alternative schools were students of color. That percentage did not matter whether the school system was predominantly black or white.

If you recall, several years ago there was a phrase used: "the school-to-prison pipeline." That pipeline—as it was mentioned in an article titled with the phrase—rings true in the lives of many of the students I served. Too often our students were categorized and identified with labels that were placed on them based solely on their past behaviors, often without the labelers even knowing the cause of the behaviors.

So, I thought, "What if we took the time to rethink how we refer to our students with a label, especially before we get to know them?"

When I think about what it means to be "at risk," it is my belief that we are all at risk every day when we walk out of our homes or even sit at home where incidents and accidents may occur. So, within this term lies a communication breakdown that can create a lack of trust.

In this book, the title of each chapter was the theme for each school year during which I served as principal in the alternative school. The goal of each year was to reach our students and build relationships with them in hopes that it would help to change the students' unknown labels.

At the end of each chapter, I ask the reader a few questions upon which to reflect. In addition, I may include action steps for you to complete on your own as self-reflection and even to share with colleagues.

It is my hope and desire that this book will help the adults supervising in our schools build positive relationships with all students, not by labeling them but rather by getting to know them.

Chapter One: Cultivating Our Chemistry

Identifying the Potential When We Work in Sync

"The meeting of two personalities is like the contact of two chemical substances; if there is any reaction, both are transformed."
— Carl Jung —

Imagine being a first-year principal with your new suit and tie. As you walk down the clean, quiet halls for the first time to check on the classrooms, you hear a loud "BOOM" then the screams of children. What do you do? Do you run down the halls and risk scuffing up your brand-new dress shoes you just got from Perry Ellis, or do you commit to that fast powerwalk similar to the people who do laps inside the mall on a Saturday morning?

Whichever action you choose, what would you do if you arrived at the classroom and saw a group of students covered in chemicals from an experiment gone wrong? Would you praise the educator for pushing the boundaries, or would you reprimand the students for not following the specific roadmap they were given at the beginning of the class?

What if I told you that this story has nothing to do with an experiment gone wrong and instead is an illustration of the relationships that administrators need to commit to developing with educators and the relationships educators need to commit to developing with students?

At the beginning of this chapter, I started with a powerful quote that I believe will guide our journey:

"The meeting of two personalities is like the contact of two chemical substances; if there is any reaction, both are transformed."

Any time two people come into a room together with their different energies and the different things they bring to the table—whether good or bad—one person or the other or both possibly can change from that interaction.

So often in the educational system, we have a multitude of energies, personalities, traditions, and ethnicities that affect the overall culture of the school, the culture of the community, and the culture of what happens in the classroom.

Just like the example I gave earlier, one negative energy or reaction can shift the whole classroom experience. It can shift the experience when a parent is doing a tour to enroll their student. It can shift the experience on test day. It can shift during the professional development opportunities we offer to our teachers as well as our students.

One of us may rub off on another to make someone else better. Or, in some cases, something we do or say when we communicate will rub off on someone else and create a negative reaction.

Cultivating our own specific chemistry is like letting chemical bonds come together to make some sort of reaction. Our chemistries will react; the challenging part is being able to manipulate the bonds in a progressive way. We need to progressively manipulate the relationships within the school community so everyone feels valued, everyone feels seen, and everyone is contributing to our students' growth.

Just like chemistry—with its overall reactions, connections, and laws and the scientific theory—we can look at the chemistry formed in educational institutions between two or more people, which is essential to growth.

So many things can be thought about in isolation. How can you grow when you're isolated? On the other hand, how do you feed off someone else? This is not to say that you can't read or watch things on your own, but when you are in fellowship, face to face with another, you get a feel of someone else's energy.

When you are in fellowship, you're able to read the energies and have multiple personalities, perspectives, and ideas weigh in. In fellowship, you're able to build upon and feed off each other's ideologies, energies, and love for the specific texts or literature you may be reading.

This is the first step in being able to build true chemistry. It begins when we think about a person's relationship with another or with specific interests they may have. A chemistry forms between the two even if they don't know each other at all. People may connect about a specific sports team or a specific stage play or show that has resonated with both.

Society has done such an intentional job of finding all the ways that divide us, all the ways to label us, and all the ways that break us apart. It shows us that we are different in so many ways. But I believe that if we look at science—chemistry specifically—and we really just take time to look at each other, we can understand that there's so much more that connects us than divides us.

I remember my first day of school as a principal. I didn't know whether the students would trust me or even whether they knew I was going to be the new principal. But I had the choice to pour out my energy, my positivity, and my perspective in a way that would progress the students forward. I didn't know what the students knew about me, but eventually our energies would connect, and it was either going to be good or bad.

How I showed up every day in the classroom—and with what I was trying to accomplish within the seats of the school—was absolutely necessary if we were going to be able to progress students forward.

I hate to say it, but judging people is sort of human nature. We are beings who should have no reason or way to judge anyone, but, truth be told, we are very judgmental. When we see a person, we're going to judge them immediately—maybe it's their attire, their actions, their speech, their dress, their mannerisms, or their look—but we may not know the true nature of that person, their story, or their struggles. Given an opportunity to get to know that person, to interact with them on an intimate basis, who knows where that can potentially go? And who knows how both of you may get your cups filled?

We all know someone or something on our own, but we know more together when we share and collaborate. When I was working on my dissertation, a gentleman in my class said he was interested in the same thing I was. He lived in Charlotte, North Carolina, and I lived in Columbia, South Carolina. We asked the professor if we would be able to complete a collaborative dissertation.

Of course, the response initially was not in our favor. The professor's reasoning was fair. He was concerned about the possibility of one of us completing more of the dissertation than the other and how he would go about giving adequate credit to the individual who deserved the most.

The gentleman and I already had come together to create a plan for implementing our collaborative effort. We explained to the professor how I was going to focus my research primarily on South Carolina, and he would examine North Carolina. After much deliberation, the professor finally agreed to allow me and this gentleman to complete a collaborative dissertation.

To ensure that we provided evidence of the collaboration, we frequently inserted quotes from the other in our respective dissertations. We also did a comparison of North Carolina and South Carolina and found many similarities and differences that added much to the project.

Again, he knew something, and I knew something, but we knew more together. I learned from him about the things being experienced in North Carolina, and he learned about the things being experienced in South Carolina. As such, we expanded our knowledge base between the two states. We didn't stop at just those two states; we studied others, but our primary focus was on North Carolina and South Carolina. To me, this was an opportunity for us to cultivate the chemistry that we had. Once we were able to sit down and talk together about our specific knowledge, we knew more together.

I jokingly tell people that because I live in Columbia, and he lives in Charlotte (and the only thing between those is Interstate 77), we would meet halfway at a Bojangles, so I often say that I learned quite a lot and earned my degree at the Chester, South Carolina, Bojangles. We would sit there with our laptops and just go at it. We pushed each other and grew because of our mutual accountability. We supported each other and did our coursework and dissertation defense in just two years.

Unfortunately, many times teachers work alone in silos—a teacher in their classroom often is solely in charge of their own domain—but because of the requirements our teachers have, they have limited opportunities to collaborate.

When I was an elementary school assistant principal, every grade level had a joint planning time; for example, all the fourth-grade teachers came together and talked about what was going on in their classrooms. At the high school and middle school levels, they might have content planning time where all the English teachers come together. These are great opportunities to collaborate and talk about the different things they're doing in their individual classrooms.

However, at the end of the day, when they go back to their classrooms, it's up to them to implement what they've talked about and learned in the discussions. Some implement things very easily; some are apprehensive about doing something because they either don't think it will work or they don't know how to implement it on their own.

Sometimes, teachers shy away from change and go back to what they know and what's familiar. It's almost like they minimize their abilities and worth and determine what they can and cannot do. They may think, "Just because this teacher can do it, does that mean I have the character? Can I pull it off?" It requires a lot of self-awareness for a teacher to identify, "Can I do this? I absolutely loved hearing this story, and I think it's a great idea, but can I do it?"

However, often when you stick with what's familiar to you, you're not going to grow. You may hear ideas you like, but if you don't implement them, you go back to where you are. What happens then is that the students also go back to where they were.

When I served as a school administrator, often there were running jokes around the school that an administrator is going to go off to this nice professional development, and he or she is going to come back with all these great ideas that teachers can implement to change the schools and the world!

What actually happens is that administrators are going to come back and ask teachers to implement these things in their classroom because they're proven to work. However, teachers become apprehensive because now the administrator has added yet another thing to their to-do lists. Sometimes, simply because of the apprehension of adding more, there's pushback and not a lot of buy-in.

In my opinion, administrators have to make sure that the new request is inclusive. Administrators need to ask, "How can we use what I've learned to add to what you're already doing?" In other words, "I don't want you to do something completely different. Let's not abandon what you're already doing, and let's not add a whole other trend to it. I want you to incorporate this new idea into what you're already doing to enhance it and make it better." It's merging the two together and blending them.

If you don't make sure that the ideas complement each other and teachers are affirmed in what they're already doing, they won't sit in front of a principal and believe in the new mission and information they're receiving. You're going to lose your audience, the teachers.

If you're an administrator reading this book, and you're going back to your classes and force feeding your teachers to implement new strategies, you're going to end up losing them. You also will end up minimizing and reducing the positive school culture you went into the school trying to implement.

We want our teachers to go back to the classroom and be effective with our students. But if they're not receiving your delivery, how effective can it be? And then how effective can it be for a student? And how effective can the relationship be we're asking our teachers and educators to build with the administrators and parents as well?

Delivery is important, and it all comes down to you taking time to empathize and consider the person and not just the profession.

The biggest thing I want you to walk away with from this chapter is that working in isolation without any interaction with other human beings is challenging.

I often tell people that I'm an only child, so if something happened or something was broken in my house, I was at fault. I knew I was at fault. But you're not the only one in a professional environment like a school. Here it's about relationships and ensuring that you're collaborating with others whether the relationship is between colleagues, between students and teachers, or even among friends and family.

On a day-to-day basis, collaboration is critical to cultivating a powerful school community, so start collaborating with others to cultivate that chemistry. It will help you begin to build the innovative school culture and classroom experience your students deserve.

When we go to a staff meeting, often teachers say it's not a gripe session, but they will talk about different concerns they have in their classrooms regarding behavior or engagement or whatever the case may be. Unfortunately, some of these things become negative.

Try changing these to more positive conversations. If you have a teacher who just sits there listening to their colleagues talk about these things, but they can't relate because they don't have those same issues, that's an opportunity for that teacher to share their positive experiences.

One year when I was principal, I asked everyone to write on a notecard what they would like to see for professional development that year or what was something they wanted to develop professionally.

Instead of me just collecting their cards and delivering the professional development, this exercise allowed them to start doing some of the research and teaching each other. They discovered that someone had a strength in something that someone else needed help with. This idea fostered a level of coteaching that made sure everyone had an active voice in it. I didn't want everything coming from me as the principal because sometimes teachers step back from that.

In the military, we learned three different styles of leadership: authoritative, delegative, and participative. Every time I've taken a leadership survey, I've always come out as being a participative leader, but I've used all three in one setting in one day.

If the superintendent or someone higher up comes and says that something needs to be done by the end of the day, I may not have time to collaborate with the staff to get their input. I may have to be authoritative and make a command decision to make it happen.

Other times, I need to use delegative leadership. When you delegate to a person, you empower them to do something and show them that you trust them and appreciate their strength. For example, my background is not in school counseling, but I can go to my school counselor, who has expertise in that particular content, and ask him or her to handle something.

But again, I default often to participative leadership, which is more collaborative. I've often had students ask me, "Why are you picking up that piece of paper?" I say, "Because it's on the floor."

Final Thoughts

I always say to give praise publicly and reprimand privately. If you're always yelling or chastising someone out loud in front of others, you're going to ruin (or at the very least damage) that relationship. If you're trying to cultivate that relationship, this is not the right direction to go.

Questions to Consider

Ask three friends to describe your relationship and how they feel about it. When these friends identify how you interact with them and give you feedback, it gives you an idea of how that relationship was cultivated within your combined chemistry. Consider how that feedback can inform a base chemistry between you and others.

Think about relationships you've seen between teachers or between administrators coming back with suggestions and their teachers. Do you have any suggestions about how teachers can be more collaborative with each other?

If 20 students come into your building with 20 different characters and 20 different personalities, they're not all going to be the same. How you engage with one student can be totally different than how you engage with another. Think about the ones you know, have concerns about, or have problems with on a regular basis, or even the ones that come in and do everything right. How do you engage with those students and continue to engage with all students?

Have a colleague or peer observe your class. After observing the class, ask that colleague, "What would you suggest and/or do to help me with my practices? Give me good advice. Give me bad advice. I want to learn from both."

How do you build positive relationships in other settings? Maybe you have a great marriage, a great friendship, or a best friend from elementary school with whom you've never skipped a beat.

How do you take those positive relationships and create the same thing in the classroom?

What are you doing in that relationship that is so great that it makes that person want to call you every week or hang out with you and still be your friend after 30 years?

How can you take some of that same energy and effort and bring it into the classroom to positively affect your students or your coworkers?

Chapter Two: Under Construction

Imperfect People Expecting Perfection from Others

"If building looks better under construction than it does when finished, then it's a failure."

— Douglas Coupland —

Don't just build and create. Don't just think and innovate. Don't just follow and act. Building, creating, thinking, innovating, following, and acting all are absolutely necessary when we're under construction.

When I think about Dr. Seuss's Whoville in *How the Grinch Stole Christmas*, all the houses looked alike, but when I think about some of the best architects and architecture—whether it's in the U.S. or another country, it's always different. It's unique to that person's specific design and point of view whether it's in the windows, the ceilings, the paintings, or the interior decor.

Whether we're building, creating, thinking, innovating, following, or acting, we're always under construction. And that means we're always growing because we're never perfect. That's fitting because what we're seeking in our classrooms and school community is not perfection; what we need to seek is progress.

I believe that every day I am blessed to wake up with another opportunity to shape students and truly show people that I am also under construction.

When writing this book, I was still a principal at one of my schools where I'd been for many years. The theme for the year was "Under Construction." As a physical example for myself and what I wanted to exemplify in the building, every classroom had large, laminated picture of a yellow hardhat on its door, and I also put them all under the entrance doors in the building with the title: "Under Construction."

My goal was for every teacher and student to walk into their classroom, see that hardhat on the door, and realize that we're not expecting perfection. I wanted everyone—which included the teachers and parents as well as the students—to come in and grow. The teacher wasn't perfect just because they were leading the classroom; they were also under construction.

If we can understand that we're all in here to grow and learn together, that's the first step to transforming an educational institution. The teacher may not fully know the content or how to best deliver it, and how they interact with different students, different personalities, and different learning levels may not be perfect, but their effort may spark something in students that can shape the rest of their lives.

Instead of trying to meet the standards, trying to be perfect, and trying to think about all the traditional ways we can do this thing we call education, let's all commit to growing together. As we commit to that growth, we rise internally as well as externally through our delivery of instruction and interactions with our school community.

I learn from the people above me and from my peers. I learn from students every single day. I've never thought anyone was beneath me. When we believe that we are all under construction, we take the first step toward really shaping a school community. If we think we're not under construction, we're sadly mistaken, fooling ourselves, and robbing our school community of what it truly needs to progress.

In education, we use the term "lifelong learner" to encourage students, but we're all lifelong learners. I want to learn more today than I knew yesterday, and I commit to that every single day. Each day is a fresh opportunity to be new, and each day is a new opportunity to grow and learn something I didn't know the day before.

I didn't want to be stagnant in my position in any way, so I had to commit to the "Under Construction" process in all things. "Tomorrow, I want to be a better husband than I was today. Tomorrow, I want to be a better dad than I was today. Tomorrow, I want to be a better supervisor than I was today. Tomorrow, I want to be a better man than I was today."

But how did I do that?

I had to reflect on and assess what I did yesterday. I had to look at the activities and decisions from the day before but not dwell on any of the faults, failings, or weaknesses. I soon came to realize what I didn't do as a part of the process, but we can't just submit to our weaknesses; we also need to celebrate our wins.

When I started to track my activities and commit to the work, I wanted to be better in every single area. I wanted to be able to sleep well at night and know that I'd given my very best. When I think about this, I think about the new opportunities I wanted to see, the new person I wanted to become, and the constant improvement that led me into the position I am in today.

We're not here just to get an evaluation from the State Department. Other people don't come in to tell us what to do. Other people aren't going to be able to measure us if we're not first measuring ourselves. That is the true challenge and mistake a lot of educators, administrators, parents, students, and building leaders make every single day. Self-measurement is what continuous improvement looks like.

We're not looking for perfection. If I come in to check a classroom or observe a class, I'm not looking for perfection from the teachers nor am I looking for perfection from the students, but I *am* looking for continuous improvement.

If I come to the same class every single day, week after week, and see that nothing has improved, that is what creates the challenge for continuous improvement and the opposition that comes across from teachers. When they do not try to implement the idea of being under construction, there is a cost. It costs your students their education, it costs parents their peace of mind, and it costs our world the bright leaders of the future who will solve the problems we've created in society today.

To this end, transparency is key. Being transparent with our students is absolutely essential to cultivating those amazing relationships that will yield success in the future. As adults, we often have the notion that because we have been in this world longer, that always makes us right. However, because we've been in this world longer, we should be wiser and better able to develop relationships that are inclusive to students' needs and not always just what we believe is right and wrong.

When you can correct yourself, admit to being wrong in certain areas, or tell a student you were wrong, that goes a long way. It shows character. It shows integrity. It shows that you're actually committed to the "Under Construction" process.

This kind of transparency is essential for building quality, authentic, and valuable relationships. There should be no limitations to your transparency; you should allow students to see your faults while also staying committed to your growth.

We have the opportunity every day to say, "You know what? I was wrong about this or that." I always tell my students, teachers, the school community, and even parents, "Hey, I got this wrong, but this is exactly what I did." So that I do not get it wrong again, I let the students know that I can own a mistake, but I also can and will do the work to teach them the process of moving forward after a mistake has been made. That helps them continue to move forward.

When I was a principal, I once facilitated a book study on

Shifting the Monkey: The Art of Protecting Good People From Liars, Criers, and Other Slackers by Todd Whitaker. Before reading and studying this book about school leadership and teacher performance, those in our study were quick to pass on their issues and responsibilities to someone else to fix or complete.

As a principal, I have no problem helping people fix issues, but generally I am not the one personally involved in the situation. For those involved, if you aren't trying to come up with a solution, don't just come up with the problem. Every time you think about bringing a problem to a specific entity, whether it's a school or the principal, I want you to consider three actions: Communicate a solution, make the punishment fit the crime, and reflect on your own limitations and imperfections.

Communicate a Solution. Offer what you can implement, or take the lead on, to get to a possible solution. This shows that you're thinking about what's in the best interest of the school, and it shows that you are forward thinking and have a vision committed to where the school can actually go. It also shows that you are continuing to support the "Under Construction" process.

Make the Punishment Fit the Crime. If I want to give a consequence to a student or staff member for an error in judgment or something they've done, I want to make sure it will be remembered, and we can grow from it.

For example, one day after we took the school flag down, a student decided to take it from where it was on a table and put it in his bookbag. I noticed it was missing the next day.

As a former soldier, I prioritized looking for the flag, but I didn't find it anywhere. I pulled the camera footage from all over the building and discovered who had taken it and where. I called in this student and let him know that I had him on camera taking the flag. He said that it had just been a joke and he'd wanted to run down the hall with it behind him like a cape.

I simply said, "Okay." When I called his mom about the behavior, it became a collaborative effort. I asked his mother, "What do you think we should do? I don't want to suspend this kid. It's not a suspension-worthy offense to me. How am I going to reach the child if he's at home on the couch missing two or three days of education? I need him in the building, but I also need him to learn how to respect the flag and not do what he did again so we both can continue to move forward."

The consequence his parents and I ended up agreeing to was that the child had to learn about the importance of the flag. We arranged with his parents that they would get him to school a little bit earlier every single morning so he could raise the flag. And they had to wait for him after school until he could lower the flag. I taught him how to properly fold the flag without showing the red of it and explained why. I also had him write a story about the history of the flag.

In regard to being "Under construction," I was building his knowledge base and trying to help him understand that even from a negative act, something positive came out of it. He learned more about the flag, how to handle it with respect, and its history all at the same time. It also taught that child that I didn't want him out of school. I needed him in the building because his education and presence were important.

Reflect on Your Own Limitations and Imperfections. Think about how you encounter the people in your life—

whether it's your students, friends, or family—on a daily basis. First, recognize that we all make mistakes, so write down three things you can do better in your life right now. We all have things we need to work on and do better. We all have areas that are currently under construction.

Face it, you are going to be under construction for the rest of your life. You're going to make mistakes. You're going to disappoint people. You're not always going to make a deadline. You're not always going to show up everywhere on time.

The reality is that you need to be transparent during these times and continue to look at those moments of making mistakes and learning lessons, so you can continue to own your "Under Construction" process and come closer to your calling.

Final Thoughts

Another "Under Construction" story involves the question of a book. At one school at which I was working, we had a "trunk or treat" event attended by more than 2,000 students that enabled us to purchase $1,500 worth of books. I had one parent call to complain about one of the books we purchased, saying that she thought the book—about a little black girl coming into a new school community—potentially promoted racism. I believed the book was about looking at how to treat children inclusively with acceptance because she was different. That parent still thought differently. This reminded me to let people know that being under construction is necessary.

We knew that students had an opportunity to grow from that book, but the pain of perception almost turned the book into a negative experience for this parent. It doesn't have to be. It never has to be negative, but sometimes we must go through uncomfortable times and seasons so we can be sure that the mission and the end of the game is still successful.

Questions to Consider

In what atmospheres do you perform better? In isolation, in small groups, in larger groups?

In what ways do you perform better?

How do you discern a student's (or colleague's) learning style?

How do you build up yourself within and how can you build up your students?

Action Steps

Take time to evaluate yourself and how you act alone in isolation. Take that same amount of time to evaluate how you act in a small group—whether of friends or colleagues—and also how you act in a larger setting of people. Record your typical actions by answering the following questions.

How did you respond by yourself?

How did you respond in the groups (small and large)?

Do you find yourself sitting in the corner, interacting, taking the lead, or sitting back and just following what is being given to you to do?

Chapter Three: Setting the Atmosphere

Controlling the Environment versus
Simply Adjusting to it

"Great leaders understand that the right attitude will set the right atmosphere, which enables the right response from others."
— John C. Maxwell —

Have you ever been going somewhere and not felt your best, but when you arrive at your destination, the energy and temperature are just right so it makes you feel a little bit better? Or perhaps, on the other end, have you ever been going somewhere and been super energized, but once you get there, it is extremely hot and there's no food that is satisfying?

This chapter is all about setting the atmosphere. I've walked into a room that's extremely hot or extremely cold, and the first thing I do is look for a way to adjust the temperature of the room or change something over which I have control—like taking off or putting on a jacket—to make myself a little bit more comfortable.

The temperature in the room relates to the atmosphere. The atmosphere doesn't always have to do with physical temperature; it could be the overall feel of the environment. How do you feel coming in? Do you feel welcome? Do you feel like you're an intruder? Do you feel like you belong? Do you feel like this is a place you should be or even would want to be? It's all about the atmosphere and your location.

As leaders, we have not only the opportunity but the responsibility to establish the atmosphere or the environment in which we live, work, and play. Leaders are largely in control of the atmosphere that their colleagues, and their students, encounter when they walk into the classroom and feel their presence. It is our responsibility as educators, administrators, and people serving an education community to establish that atmosphere.

When you are an administrator or a teacher, are you the thermostat or are you the thermometer? The first part is being able to differentiate between the two. A thermostat sets the temperature (or atmosphere); the thermometer just measures what has already been set.

At the end of the day, you're either going to be the thermostat or the thermometer. I encourage us, as leaders, to be the thermostat that sets the tone for the classroom or meeting or whatever space you're in. If you have that responsibility and you enter a room to find that it's not what you deem appropriate, determine the possibilities and assess what opportunities you have to affect the atmosphere.

A teacher or administrator in a leadership capacity absolutely must have that authority or presence about them wherever they go. It creates a comfortable environment and makes people want to be there.

You can think about the atmosphere as curb appeal. If an event is at a particular building or school, we have to ensure that when a parent walks into our school—even as soon as they park their car—they have an opportunity to size up the grounds to see how much we care about our school. Are the grounds well kept? Is the property clear of debris and hazards? Once they walk into the building, are they greeted as though they belong there? Or are they treated as though someone has to stop what they're doing to monitor the guests?

Ultimately, that is your first opportunity to make an impression. You can't make a second one. When they walk through the door, they're going to come in and see what they see, hear what they hear, and feel what they feel.

To quote the great late Dr. Maya Angelou:

"I've learned that people will forget what you said, people will forget what you did, but people will never forget how you made them feel."

Just think about that. You may have a conversation with

someone, and you may remember the entire conversation, but you may not remember certain parts of the conversation when you walk away. But you will walk away feeling happy, sad, angry, nervous, or anxious—that's the presence you have with that person or in that environment.

You remember the feeling of the encounter much more than the words being used. That feeling is going to go much further than the words, but words also can create in you the feeling that you want, or do not want, to go back and speak to that person at another time.

Of course, this can go well or badly. "You know when we talked last week, I was so motivated by our conversation!" "Well, you know, I walked away a little bit upset because you brought up some things that I didn't realize were going to make me feel poorly when we interacted."

Back in Chapter One, we talked about cultivating our chemistry. When you interact with a person, or several people, with each person's chemicals joining together, everyone is going to react in some way. That reaction can tie into the atmosphere that was set.

I implore you to be the person taking the opportunity and understanding their responsibility in setting the atmosphere. It can be positive or negative depending on what outcome you want for that particular encounter. You have control over the environment, and it's up to you to ensure that your choices, actions, and behaviors are in alignment with the vision you actually want for your school culture.

When I think of the research and the quote by Dr. Angelou, which has resonated with me over and over again, I think about when I've done character surveys in the past. Every time, it tells me that I'm a person who likes to connect with people to make them feel good about themselves. I like to empower and develop people.

I've identified that about myself, and I encourage you to do the same for yourself if you haven't already. Identify qualities about yourself. If you have weaknesses that you want to turn into strengths, I want you to take intentional action steps to ensure that you know who you are and feel good about who you are. You also need to make sure that your weaknesses aren't detrimental to the experience and atmosphere provided to other people.

This role, or the room itself, can be very comfortable, but you still might feel uncomfortable. Could it be because of how someone speaks to you or how someone's body language interacts with yours? Think about the students that come into your class. Can you imagine what the students feel coming into your environment or atmosphere?

I'm not going to pretend they're all coming in happy and skipping and jolly, but if you think about them coming in that way, it sets the tone that this could be a positive day.

Imagine the kid who barely comes in the door, dragging his bookbag or jacket then flopping down into the chair and immediately putting his head on the desk. The atmosphere into which that student walks can affect him, but right now perhaps they're anxious and bent on setting the atmosphere for others.

How do we, as adults, encounter that student who comes into our classroom not so happy or not wanting to be there? How do we motivate them? What do we do with the students to make them actually want to be there?

Of course, outside elements potentially affect those students; they affect us all. How many of us, as teachers and administrators, have walked in with that same dragged-down energy that shows our students we don't want to be there and aren't ready for the day?

Have you ever heard the phrase "Fake it 'til you make it"? The reality is that you have to stop "faking it until you make it" and check your negative energy at the door. Everyone experiences certain times that make them feel like they have to fake it, but the real goal is to walk around more positively, more progressively, and more purposefully so we can exude that power in our classrooms and within our school culture.

The reality of our lives may not be perfect, but how we view and show others our lives may be the very determining factor that shapes the rest of our school culture, the school experience, and our students' education.

Can you change the atmosphere for that one student? Can you change the atmosphere for that one teacher? Can you change the atmosphere for that one administrator? Changing the atmosphere for that individual does not necessarily mean you have to change the atmosphere for all. But is it possible that changing the atmosphere for one might change it for others as well? It's very possible.

This is in line with talking about the differentiation of instruction, how students learn, and how students are affected by that interactions, feelings, and culture as well. If you have ever traveled outside the United States, you know that wherever someone is from—whether it's South America or the Middle East—they bring with them certain cultures or traditions. That's the same in the classroom. We have to be very mindful that even the backgrounds and cultures among Americans—Caucasian, African, Latino, Asian—are different and embedded within each individual from their part of the world.

When you go into a household with a nationality different from your own, the atmosphere you walk into could be somewhat uncomfortable for you, and you have to try to fit in. A common saying is to "get in where you fit in," but you need to help create that sense of being comfortable for others.

In a perfect world and classroom environment, students come in energetic, happy, ready to learn, and excited about learning. They sit down with their books out and eyes and ears open, focusing on the teacher. That's a perfect scenario, but it's not often reality. In so many cases, it's not even the reality from one class period to another. Your first class of the day may be completely different from your last class of the day, and your second class comes in and challenges every fiber in your being.

There's a saying among teachers and educators that may not be great, but in the vein of being as transparent as possible may resonate with you. Teachers will sometimes refer to their "Hell period," meaning that a particular class or class period has the reputation and history of being problematic on a regular basis. For these classes, teachers are already setting themselves up to embrace and share an atmosphere of disdain, like, "Oh my god, here we go." We downright dread that particular period or class coming in.

But instead of dreading that "Hell period," why not try to shift and establish a new atmosphere? How can we get that atmosphere to be different?

Granted, students might be better in a different subject or are at a different level or have a different caliber, but maybe it's time to sit back evaluate how and why your other periods are more successful. Even if there are different students, you're experiencing a level of success with other classes. What makes it successful? Have you tried those same actions or tactics with the "Hell period"? See if you can bring those differences over. Once you do, you possibly can change and set a better atmosphere for that problematic class, so it is more conducive to being the learning environment you desire.

Who wins with this change? The teacher? Yes. But more so, the students win, and learning takes place. Will it be perfect every day? Of course not. We have to work at this on a regular basis.

We also want to ask students to buy in. "How do you feel about this class? Why is it that we come in and have this trouble every day? What's going on in this particular class?" Getting the students' buy-in by hearing their voices is essential. Many times, as adults, we make all the decisions, choices, and moves without ever conferring with the children, but the main people affected by what we do every single day are those children. They should have a stake.

I'm still trying to understand how we expect to grow and move forward in our careers and in our craft when the people we are trying to affect don't have a voice. When you hear from them, take notice of their voices, and interact with them the way you should, you will be amazed. Once you encounter that kid and hear their voice, and even, if possible, implement their voice into your actions or behaviors, you are going to win that student over, and that atmosphere is going to change.

That brings me to a story when I served as a principal of a charter school in South Carolina. When I entered the school, the hours of operation for student attendance were very loose—I mean extremely loose. Students only had to come to school for a few hours a week. It was a hybrid school, so they had access to the school 24/7 via a computer, but they only had to be in the building for four hours a week. They had free reign to choose those four hours and the days they came in as long as they were in the building on two days for a total of four hours. For example, a student could come on a Monday from 10 a.m.–12 p.m. and come back on Thursday from 1–3 p.m.

However, you always get out of something what you put into it. Just imagine the atmosphere of that school where students were talking to their peers and encouraging them to come to this school because of the relaxed schedule and the opportunity to come and go and do as they pleased.

When I became the principal of that school, the academics were failing. I promptly associated the poor academics with the environment. There was no accountability and no guarantee that students would come in and show their abilities to the teacher on a consistent basis. It was come and go, come and go, come and go with no tracking nor accountability.

I remember that when I interviewed for the job, I walked down the hall to the conference room and students were just walking down the hall. There was no bell schedule, nothing to tell them to move to the next period. If a student came and sat in one chair for 10 minutes and didn't like that classroom, they could go someplace else for 10 minutes or they could sit in the hallway. There was no accountability.

I immediately sat down and tried to think about how I was going to restructure the accountability of students coming to school on a consistent basis with more of a routine. Since the school was different than a traditional school, I knew I couldn't take them straight to a traditional school model, but I knew that if we continued doing what we were doing, the school definitely would fail academically in every aspect.

The school was designed to support students who had

struggles in their home lives. Some had to work to help out at home. Some were teenage parents who did not have the opportunity or desire to be in school all day. A lot of students, just being teenagers with short attention spans, just had a hard time being in a structured setting all day.

I had to decide whether I wanted students to be in the school in the morning or the afternoon, so I came up with a schedule. I knew that changing the schedule would change the entire atmosphere of the school, and I knew that students who were there since before me were used to coming in and going as they wished. But I shared my thoughts and the reasons I wanted to make the hours more consistent with certain students. I went to the cafeteria and said, "Hey, I'm looking at changing the schedule as it relates to how you come in."

Of course, I had pushback from some who were used to the very loose schedule and didn't want to go back to anything structured. I also used the opportunity to get input about what it looked like for them as students. What did they want?

I had a student come up with an idea that made me think and wonder, and, by the end of the day, her solution made more sense than mine. On one hand, I currently had an extreme structure that was too loose, but my alternative extreme might have been too much of a change.

This student shared with me a solution that she thought would be great, and I implemented it in school. For the next four years, that was the school's schedule. It went from two days and four hours per week to having students come in Monday through Thursday for four hours in the morning or four hours an afternoon. They still didn't have to stay all day, but the half day they had to give me was at their discretion—either in the morning or afternoon.

Here again, I gave the students some choice and input. If a student was not a morning person or worked a shift from which they got off late, they wouldn't have to get up in the morning. They could take the afternoon class then leave school and go straight to work. Alternatively, if they wanted to get their school commitment out of the way and then go to work, they had that opportunity and option as well.

During the students' self-selected four hours, they had structured time to sit with an English teacher for an hour, a math teacher for an hour, a science teacher for an hour, and an elective course teacher for an hour. They did that but also knew that, with a hybrid environment, the expectation outside of school was that they would continue their assignments. This schedule allowed students the flexibility they needed and desired.

Students with that new schedule graduated in three years. I even had one who graduated in two years flat. The former structure did not require seat time, so they didn't have to be in the class at a certain time. It was only about competency and meeting the requirements in their subject matter to get credit. The new atmosphere had students coming up to me, saying, "I heard I could come here to catch up."

The atmosphere of the loose school where students could just come and go as they pleased had them barely getting by if graduating at all. With that model, the graduation rate had gone down to 25%, and state law required it to be 70% minimum.

When I came into the school, we implemented the changes that altered that atmosphere of accountability. In the conference room, we even made a data wall on which students could come and see their names color-coded to show them their credits and progress at their grade level. They were able to see instantly how they were progressing. Once they finished one class and then another, they began to feel successful. That opportunity changed not only the atmosphere of the building but the atmosphere of their belief in themselves. They started to change when they could see things moving in a positive manner, and we started to win over the students.

Making slight changes as simple as a schedule shifted the entire atmosphere of the building. Now students wanted to come to my school because they understood that here they could get caught up and get back to their right grade and graduate on time or even ahead of time.

The popularity started there, and, within the first two years, the graduation rate went from 29% to 61%. We doubled the graduation rate simply because we established an atmosphere of accountability. Because of the data wall, we knew our kids by name and face and grades. We had real conversations. The atmosphere of caring for them quickly told us that they felt we cared about them and tried to work with them at the school.

Of course, sometimes you face opposition when you go into a school and start making changes. Parents sometimes push back at it. The students definitely push back at it. I've even had to work on this with the teachers. But our job as educators is to support our students and get them back on track and where they need to be.

In this school, we needed to change the mindset of our expectations. As such, the atmosphere could not just be changed by me. I certainly could lead the charge of the change, but I needed my teachers to support it. They were the ones in the trenches, the ones who were doing it, so I shared with them the student's idea, and the teachers loved it. It gave them a chance to work with a specific group of students in the morning and a different group of students in the afternoon.

They also had 45 minutes in the middle of the day to eat lunch together, cultivate their colleague chemistry, collaborate, and talk about certain students and how they've supported them and what support they may still need. That was essential because we were all still building on what we could do better to improve our school and set an atmosphere for when students come into the school.

After the change, we had fewer attendance issues because they wanted to come in and wanted to be there. They knew they only had to be there for four hours, whereas the traditional school required 6–7½, and they still were able to get the same curriculum and work on their own. That enticed a lot of them.

When the kids left our halls, they could go off to college where the average student does not have a full day every day. College students set their schedule to avoid morning classes, to be done before noon, to take evening classes, or even to pick classes only on Tuesdays and Thursdays. The opportunity to set a schedule in college is ideal. Having the schedule that we did exposed them to that opportunity early, so we were even giving them a head start on the reality of college.

Of course, coming out of college, you go to work and back to a full-time day. But by that point, you must measure those motivations within yourself, know your strengths and weaknesses, and know what you have to do to ensure your own success.

Final Thoughts

An environment affects those within it, so it is very important to foster the proper setting to be productive and have positive growth. An environment can be positive and set people up for success, or it can be negative and drag people down. We must set the atmosphere that makes students want to be there and be positive and successful.

As educators, we have heard probably 100 times that kids don't care how much you know until they know how much you care. That's true. We must give genuine respect to our kids and show that we care for them.

I ask you to constantly think of your students' behavior and how they enter your classroom as well as how staff members enter a room for a meeting. Document those findings. Do students come in happy and chipper with a little pep in their step? Do your colleagues drag themselves into a staff meeting after a long day, or do they come in energetic and ready to learn and share about their day?

The Internet provides many opportunities for us to glean knowledge from what we see and hear, so I encourage you to seek out and watch two or three videos related to classroom management. Find 2–3 positives and 2–3 negatives.

Questions to Consider

Do people gravitate to you?

How do you set the tone for your class or your office?

Do you come in with high expectations and high energy?

Do you come in with nonchalant, low energy as the leader of that space?

If someone else sets the tone through their behavior or actions, how do you regain it? How do you adjust?

How do you get the atmosphere back on track the way you want it to be?

How do you get children excited to learn or coworkers to want to be attentive and hear your story?

How do you differentiate between being a thermostat and a thermometer?

How do you gain and give respect to others?

Chapter Four: Lead from Where You Are

Not Having to Be the Leader to Lead

"Leadership is the art of giving people a platform for spreading ideas that work."
— Seth Godin —

For years, society has battled with effectively defining "authentic leadership." This challenge is not exclusive to education; it is also found in the private sector, in our homes, and throughout the country and the world.

As we think about leadership, we first must think about good leadership qualities. Qualities, such as integrity, honesty, progressive thinking, problem-solving ability, and many others are expected in a true leader.

But the real question is, "How do you define leadership?" Are you the leader that your students, your school, and your school community need? If not, have you ever reflected on why that may be?

You may have heard the saying, "Lead, follow, or get out of the way." A person who is a natural leader will take over, they will lead, and people will want to follow them.

I learned from 20 years in the military that leadership is the art of influencing others to accomplish a mission. Even 18 years after having retired from service, that still resonates in my mind as the definition of leadership, and I often use it in interviews when I'm asked how I define leadership.

People want to follow a good leader, but there is a difference between leadership and management. Some people replace someone in management and earn that title simply by how long they've been there. But a "leader" is someone who people want to follow. People see something in them that they want to emulate. They want to take advantage of being in the presence of a great leader.

Do you have to be in a leadership capacity by title to be considered a leader? Of course not. Some people don't want to follow a manager, so they lead from where they are. Leadership is in all of us. Here are some other questions to ponder. Are leaders born? Are they created? Can you learn to be a leader?

If you consider yourself a leader, what do you think about yourself? Do you feel that you've learned to do something through the years and have expertise? Do you think it's something with which you were born? How did you feel about being on the playground as a child when it came to picking teams or deciding what you were going to do in the garden or in your house playing with siblings? Who took over and showed leadership in them? Did it have to do with being the oldest child, the middle child, or the youngest?

Truly there is no age specific to leadership nor is there a race or gender. Leadership is leadership, and it's disappointing to think that, even in America today, we hear about the glass ceiling where women do not have the same opportunities as a man, or, if they do, the pay isn't equal. I'm just glad to see that some of those ceilings are being broken.

But even with the glass ceiling, is their leadership any different? Leadership by a woman may even be substantially better and yet isn't acknowledged as such, so it is important to lead from where you are and think about what you do in your capacity.

One year in my school, I did a book study on *The 360-Degree Leader: Developing Your Influence from Anywhere in the Organization* by John C. Maxwell. From that book, we learned to lead up, lead down, and lead across.

Leading up is when the teacher supports an administrator or assistant principal. Just because the administrator is in a position of authority does not mean teachers can't share ideas and information with them that may be very helpful to the situation at hand. If an administrator asks you to do a particular task with your class, but you know a better, more efficient, or more effective way to do it to get a more significant outcome, share that with the administrator as a suggestion based on your previous practices or knowledge. That's leading up. Hopefully, the person in leadership is open to that and understands the validity of your contribution.

Leading down is when a classroom teacher is put in charge of a classroom. The instructor determines what goes on during the day as the leader of that classroom.

Leading across is speaking with colleagues or engaging in standard planning periods, perhaps during lunch, to give and get advice about things they struggle with or have success with. You can be a leader in this capacity among peers by giving ideas, input, and support.

Leading up is just as important when working with students; for example, when I took the advice of a student to change the schedule for how students attended class (Chapter Three). I'm the leader of the school, but that didn't mean I couldn't listen to a student and her voice. That gave her a sense of leadership. She stood up and suggested something to me, and I made sure that I shared with her classmates across the school that the new schedule we were adopting came from one of their peers.

From this, you can see that when students are allowed to have a voice and have that voice implemented in a big way, they see that their point of view and input matter and might be executed at times. If their input isn't used completely, that doesn't mean it was terrible. It may just not be appropriate for that moment or particular time. In that case, I would simply share with the student, "I like your idea. It may not fit at this moment, but I'm going to consider it. Let's talk about it later."

This perfectly illustrates leading from where you are. If a student comes to you with something, we need to embrace that. Many students—and many people in general—don't do that. Some people just go with the flow, going along to get along and never speaking up.

But there's so much potential in so many of us. We just have to make sure that we can get ourselves around the right people, in the right environment, with the right opportunities to grow.

As we continue to talk about leading from where you are, consider that everyone has both strengths and weaknesses. No one is just overflowing with strengths, and none of us are just stuck in weakness. But there is some of both in every single human being.

We tend to operate within our strengths because they are more prevalent, make us cheerful, and bring about the good in us. But we shouldn't constantly focus on our strengths. You don't want lose sight of your fortes, but don't overexaggerate them and overlook the weaknesses, especially if we have disadvantages that go unaddressed.

How can those be strengthened? How do we get better? How can we overcome them? We need to take time to look at our weaknesses, and we need to find people who will help us build us up in those weaknesses and hopefully turn them into strengths. Power is found in strengthening our areas of imperfection. That makes us better and more productive overall.

Think about areas of your life you consider weaknesses. Are they in your work or your relationships? Do they bother you? Would you like to improve on them to enhance your life? If you answered yes to any of these questions, congratulations.

Growth is on the way.

In the meantime, lead from where you are in your strengths while you are working to improve your weaknesses. Consider the saying that a chain is only as strong as its weakest link. Does that weak link have to remain weak? Or can that chain (or in our case a team) be built up or helped to become better? And why can't the chain be strong throughout you?

When thinking that a team is only as strong as its weakest link, that link may be referring to someone you may feel doesn't need to be a part of the team or does not bring much to the team. But the risk there is dismissing the potential leadership in that person. Not everyone has the same level of strengths or weaknesses, and that person could grow into a leader or an even better leader than the original one.

I've talked to many teachers in my 18 years in education who would tell me that they can't do administration. "I don't want the headaches. I don't want this. I don't want that." I respect that because everyone may not want to be in that kind of leadership capacity.

But I tell this to my teachers all the time. All of us are leaders. You are the leader of your classroom. When you are in that classroom with those 20–30 students, they look up to you as the adult and leader in that room. I'm down the hall in my office doing what I do, and I come in periodically, but you are the leader in that classroom.

I also want them to look around that classroom and the school at all the different personalities there. There are leaders rising in that school. Is it the person who answers the most questions, helps the most, participates the most, gets classmates to quiet down when they need to be quiet, or gets a conversation started when you need one? Maybe. We never know where that leader is coming from and in what way.

Sometimes we see a person as quiet or timid, but, in the right atmosphere, with the right opportunity and the right push, who knows what can come out of them. A quiet person who sits in the corner never really speaking to their peers could be the next budding senator, governor, or even president of the United States.

We must take into consideration that anyone can lead from where they are. If you watch students, even in kindergarten when they're playing house or store, one or several of them will display leadership ability. They're going to take charge. Someone always wants to be the one who runs the store. That kid is exuding their leadership in their actions during simple play.

We're the same way as adults. We are all still trying to find our place in the world and where we can be a leader. Through society's eyes, men are supposed to be the leaders of their homes, but how many of us have been in households where the male presence is absent? I, for one, grew up with my mom as a single mother. I didn't have a father figure in my house to show me the ways to be a husband, a dad, or the man of the house. I had to learn those things through others, and I did it vicariously by watching what others were doing on television, absorbing things I read, and sometimes by experiencing them the hard way.

I got married at a relatively young age; I was only 20 years old, and my wife was 18. Suddenly, I was the man of my house, which came with certain expectations. I'm not saying that a man leads a woman or a woman leads a man, but we have different things we do together to share the load.

This also applies to working together in a classroom. When

students are in small groups, we will ask someone to take the lead and perhaps generate the conversation. Giving out roles to different students provides leadership opportunities for everyone in the group to do their part. Leadership doesn't always have to be in the hands of just one person at any one time.

Think about the opinions you may have. Think about the different people under whom you have worked, different teachers you've had, or different supervisors you've had. Think about their leadership. Was that person you wanted to follow a genuine, good leader? Did they give you the feeling that, in your capacity or position at the time, you were also a leader and your voice and work were worthy and desired? Those are ways of thinking about how you lead from where you are.

Also keep asking yourself the right questions. Am I happy? Compared to where I am now, can I do better? What position should I be seeking to best exude my leadership?

I retired from the military in 1985. After 20 years of service, many of those in a leadership capacity were noncommissioned officers. When I went into the classroom, I felt like my leadership experience from my military life affected students positively.

After a few years, I wanted to go into administration because I thought, "If I can affect a classroom like this, how much better could I affect a school as an administrator?" So, in my fourth year in education, I moved into administration to do just that. I had some success, and that put me on a path in my next year to become the principal of a school.

Five years out of the military, and I went from being a classroom teacher to an assistant principal to a principal. I saw a leadership in myself that I wanted to show to others and share in a different light from a different capacity. As such, I stepped out of my comfort zone to make those moves.

Again, think of where you are. Think of what you do. You know your strengths. You know your weaknesses. Don't be afraid to step out and show that. Many people don't think they have leadership abilities, but that often is because no one—perhaps not even themselves—has tapped into it or an opportunity hasn't presented itself.

As classroom teachers, we need to give the students who seem least likely to be considered leaders the chance to lead. We have to look at the potential in people, seeing not just where they are but their potential to be better than us and move through anything and everything.

Leadership is always going to come with some opposition, but that is part of it. Think about Moses leading people through the Red Sea. Think about Jesus. There was something about Moses and Jesus that people wanted to follow, and they had the opportunity to show their leadership.

Does everyone have the ability to lead people like this? Maybe they can, but for whatever reason, perhaps they've never risen to the occasion and done it.

Think about people in politics. They come through the ranks as attorneys then as local politicians then they take it to the national stage to be high-profile politicians. As of the Biden-Harris administration, we now can applaud the United States for having its first woman—and woman of color—leading as vice president, the second in command for the entire United States.

Imagine that you had the chance to talk to Kamala Harris and find out what she was like at home as a three-year-old or five-year-old playing with her sister, or how she was as a young girl at school or at recess or helping in the classroom. How was she in high school and in college and in her adult life? Consider all the different levels and transitions she had to make in her leadership styles on that path to becoming the Vice President of the United States of America.

Then think about your own experiences. Have you ever been called on by the teacher to lead something or been made the team captain? Did your friends look to you and say that you're the one they want doing it? Do you have that natural knack to say that you'll do it? If so, that was you stepping outside your box to be a leader.

Final Thoughts

Everyone can lead at any given time, so the key thing to remember is that you need to lead from where you are.

Have you put yourself in a box? Are you hiding your potential? Are you able to see potential in others to ensure that they also can come out from where they are to be great leaders in our schools, in our society, or in our environment?

Don't sell yourself short, and don't sell others short. Seek potential in others. Bring it out, highlight it, and let's grow together.

Questions to Consider

What characteristics do your students or teams see when they see you?

Do you see yourself as a leader? If yes, why do you see yourself as a leader? If not, why do you not see yourself as a leader?

Do you know and understand your strengths and weaknesses?

How can you build your leadership capacity and that of others?

Chapter Five: Character Check

Ensuring that the Image in the Mirror Is Right First

"Weakness of attitude becomes weakness of character."
— Albert Einstein —

Often, we need to understand not only who we think we are but also who others think we are. Think back to the song "Man in the Mirror" recorded by the late Michael Jackson. The lyrics convey that there are times when we need to look into the mirror to find out who we are. It's straightforward to think we're one thing but then we might be perceived differently by those with whom we interact daily.

As we continue to learn how to influence our students, consider how you think about supporting them, getting them on the right track, and helping them with the behaviors we may not be very fond of?

We look at our students and think about what we see in them or what we think of them, but they are also evaluating us, so we must take the opportunity to look in the mirror and think about our character and what we bring to the table.

John Wooden said:

> *"Be more concerned with your character than your reputation*
> *because your character is what you really are*
> *while your reputation is merely what others think you are."*

So again, look in the mirror.

Often, you want to leave somewhere with a reputation. "I want to be known as this. I want to be known as having done that." But do you want that reputation to precede you for what you've done or for what people think of you? Or do you want your character to be at the forefront of your life, identifying not what people think of you but who you really are?

I have another quote on a gift I received from students when I was principal of the alternative school, and I have had it on my desk at work for years. Lao Tzu says:

"Watch your thoughts, they become your words; watch your words, they become your actions; watch your actions, they become your habits; watch your habits, they become your character; watch your character, it becomes your destiny."

Even at their beginning, our thoughts can create our destiny because they create the feeling of what people think of us. After all, those thoughts are going to come out in words and then become actions. Actions are the key. When people see you in action, you either become who they think you are, or they come to know who you are.

We have also heard a lot that actions speak louder than words. Think about your character and the actions you have. We can look a certain way on paper, but we also can have a reputation from which people perceive us. We often create that reputation by doing great things in the company of others, but it's when people are not watching that your character is defined.

As a school principal, I often used to say that I could not leave my house and go to the local department store or a restaurant with friends and act out of character because I never knew when my students or a student's parent will see me, and my reputation and my character intertwine.

If I am not conscious of it, they may start to say, "Oh, I noticed your principal at this location during this particular event or doing something that was 'out of character' or 'outside of the expectation' of how a principal should be."

One of my former colleagues, now a superintendent, said that the only place he was never a principal was in his house. When he left his home, everywhere he went was an opportunity to run into a student or a parent that he had served over the years. What they saw him do in his actions or even heard him say during those actions laid the foundation of what they thought of him or his character. We all know it goes back to making first impressions, and you can't make a first impression the second time around.

We need to be mindful about what we expect, or want, people to think of us, but the other question is whether you care. My answer is that we should care because our character goes a long way. Your nature can, as quoted, lead you to your destiny.

I quoted her earlier, but it's worth repeating Dr. Maya Angelou:

"When people show you who they are, believe them the first time."

First impressions are lasting ones, so can you reinvent yourself if your first impression is not well received? Is there a second chance to make that first impression?

When Dr. Angelou says that people show you who they are the first time, that's an indication right there. Someone has identified your character based on your actions. It could be the first time they have seen you, and they may not know you. They may never get the chance to know you based on the potential of your relationship or your connectivity throughout time. If that person does not get the opportunity to know the real you, the representation you share with them upfront is what they know and will go with. That's what you have modeled for them to take away from the table. It's what they have in their head.

Is this any different than our students' first day of school? The first time they meet the teacher or the first time the teacher meets the students, do we size them up? Do we try to identify or attach a character to them at the onset of our meeting? Should we give them the benefit of the doubt and get to know them as people? Of course, we should give everyone the chance for us to get to know them so we can understand who they are and maybe even why they are how they are.

But often we don't allow it to go that far. We immediately place some tag or label that attaches a character to that person. It could be great, but then the person does not live up to it. It could be harmful, and the person is not able to make it better.

Nevertheless, whatever character trait we see in that person stood out in our minds for some time. Some people come out of that quickly, but Stephen M. R. Covey, in his book, *Speed of Trust: The One Thing That Changes Everything*, says:

"You can't talk your way out of a problem you behaved your way into."

In other words, you conducted yourself into that behavior, and those actions speak louder than words.

You also have heard that a picture is worth 1,000 words. Sometimes when those actions are conveyed—whether good, bad, or indifferent—a person will walk away from that interaction and think and consider something or attach a quality to your name.

If we want to assure others that our character is of good essence, we may wish to review it as we walk into the school building. Our colleagues see our actions and how we interact with children. The parents may see how you interact with their child. Right then, they are sizing us up. They are attaching a character to us.

A parent can see you interacting with a child and showing genuine care, concern, and love and say, "I liked that this teacher seems to have my child's best interests at heart." Or a colleague can say, "Wow, I love how Mr. or Mrs. so and so interacts with their children, how they meet them at the door, how they interact with them in the classroom when doing a lesson, or even in the hallway or during free time in the cafeteria."

That builds relationships. That teacher starts to build not only a reputation but a character. If your character can override reputation, you're winning. Let your character and your actions speak for you, and let your actions be the things that give you the opportunity to show who you are to everyone you with whom you interact.

I think of it like this: I am who I am, but can I be someone else? Should I try to be someone else? Is my authentic self always my best representation? Is it the best one I can present to others?

We must consider our environment and those over whom we have a sphere of influence. If our character is flawed, those flaws very well could have a negative impact or effect on those we are around.

If we are going to encourage, motivate, mentor, guide, and lead our children to be lifelong learners and good citizens in our community, how can we take them there when our character doesn't show them that we're there? The very thing we're trying to get our children to do is look in the mirror.

Personally, I'm implementing, exercising, and showing up in my actions when I walk and talk. We can't talk one way and show a different side. We must walk our talk to be true to ourselves and deliver our true character to others.

Many people operate daily behind a fake persona and are not portraying or describing who they really are. Of course, people have their home life and their work life. I understand and respect that we should separate the two. Who I am at work may not exactly be who I am at home, but I also need to realize that who I am at home can bleed over into work. I am not just the teacher or the principal. I am me, and I am who I am as an individual. When I hang out with my friends or family, I also need to realize that if I'm in a public place, it's an opportunity to be seen by those from my workplace to whom I want to show good character. If they see me outside work, would what I do make my character null and void? "I thought they were like this, but when I saw them over here…"

When you think about life and death, think about the year of your birth. For example, let's say you were born in 1970, the year of your death could be 2060. If you look at a headstone or an obituary, you see the Alpha and the Omega of it by the dates, but what is in that dash in the middle? We know the beginning, and we can speculate on the end date, but what is your story in the middle? Is it that a pupil can say you were a great person who always represented himself in a particular manner of character?

We think about somebody's reputation, and your character can support your reputation very well. But remember, your reputation is how people see you; your character is who you are. If you are true to yourself and display your character consistently, it's going to lead toward you having an excellent reputation.

Great character is of great importance, but the two are still different. Think about things you have said in the past or things you have done by your actions. How many of us say, "Oh man, I regret ever doing this. I regret doing that," especially if there were people involved?

Someone recently said to me that anyone who's over 40 can point out the biggest difference between their childhood, teenage years, and young adulthood versus today is that it was before the advent of social media and widespread technology. Nowadays everything is recorded. Everything is streamed. Everything is shown and shared on social media. We need to be very mindful of the things we post. Although you may not friend your students or colleagues on social media platforms, that doesn't mean they cannot see who you are and what you're doing outside of your job. Your character is a very, very important part of your person.

We didn't have recording devices at the ready during that time. We didn't have social media. Despite so many things we likely did, and our character was somewhat protected because it was only done or known about in a small circle. Now, when you do something, especially if it's negative, your behavior and character can be displayed across the county, the state, or even worldwide, depending upon the behavior.

Today, we need to be extra mindful that although it can take just a second to show great character, it can take even less than a split second to ruin your reputation through your actions.

Think about when you stand in the grocery store check-out ailse and you notice the magazines on the rack. Even though you have the state newspaper and things like *The New York Post* telling you national news or events and things happening in your community, so many times, we are attracted to the garbage. We are drawn to negativity. Many times, we look at *The Globe* or *The Enquirer* and see all the negative stories about a person. We see it in the headlines or on the front page, but we don't really know the truth. The next thing you know, it enters the rumor mill, and we gossip about celebrities we don't even know.

That's the same thing as one of your students or colleagues seeing you in a place that they may not think was appropriate and you exhibiting a particular behavior they may feel doesn't fit either. So right there, they're looking at you through the eyes of *The Enquirer* or *The Globe* instead of looking at the whole story's true details in your local newspaper to understand what's going on. From there, can you come back to your true story to protect or rebuild your character?

I am not saying that you can't do it, but it is tough to rebuild or regain something that's already put out into the atmosphere. It goes back to the quote from Stephen Covey's book that you can't talk yourself out of something you've put yourself in, especially regarding oppositions and challenges with character checks.

We often hear someone say, "I'm an adult. I'm grown. I have the right to do whatever, and be whoever, I want to be outside of my job. But even so, we are still a representation of our workplace, depending on the career field you're in.

We need to be mindful. I can't go out and just say or do anything and think that my words are not going to be impactful to a parent or a subordinate or a colleague. I can't think that those words or actions, just because I'm off work or off duty, do not still go back to my job. There's still an expectation.

In my 20 years of service in the military, there were certain things about which I had to be mindful as a soldier. I belonged to the United States Army. If you recall the G.I. Joe dolls, many of us did not realize that the "G.I." stood for "Government Issue." So, when you, as a soldier, sign on the dotted line, you become government property, and you are representing the military and the federal government in your voice, actions, and behavior every time you walk out of your home, especially if you are in uniform or someone knows you are in the military.

I can also break this down to our household thinking when considering our students. As adults in the building, we often say that the children we serve are products of their homes. So, their character often is built off what we think has happened at their homes. If we see a particular behavior or hear specific language or conversations from them at school or in public, we immediately tie it back to what was learned at home. It could very well be so, and we need to think about that.

As educators, many of us have children of our own. We may think we're off work or off duty and it is our time, but we need to act and carry ourselves a certain way while at home around our children. When they go to school, do your children represent you in a particular way that keeps your character intact, or do you have to be concerned? The bottom line is that we should not judge our students by their homes. We may see some connections to the behaviors from their situation, but that doesn't necessarily have to define that child.

Again, the character that people see may or may not be what you want to portray, so we need to be extremely careful about how we convey things to one another.

I remember one time when I was in the military as a young soldier, maybe even less than a year in, and I was not happy with some things going on in my unit. I was having a conversation about what was going on, and it wasn't positive. That got back to the battalion commander, and I found myself called on the carpet and being told about the sense of loyalty that I had betrayed. He said that if there was anything I did not like or desire in my unit, it was not for me to take that outside of the team. Things needed to be settled and cared for and honored and respected within the organization.

That takes me back to the book *Speed of Trust*. When you betray that trust, just as I had broken the trust of my battalion commander by talking negatively about an activity we'd done, it is challenging to get that trust back.

That action hurt my reputation and my character. I very well could have been seen as untrustworthy and was going to speak negatively of our unit outside the building from then on.

Final Thoughts

Think of that and reflect on your character: the "man in the mirror." Watch your thoughts and know that even our thoughts, if we are not careful, are going to be implemented and show as our character. When that character is identified, that can and will become your destiny.

You could be overlooked for a promotion or not even get an opportunity to interview with a particular organization because your character preceded you to the person who was making the decision. It could be very detrimental to your purpose in moving forward.

Self-evaluate who the person is that you present to others during interactions. By doing so, you also will understand others more. Do you want someone to see you without giving you a chance? Think about that as you interact with people. Do you get to know the person, or do you categorize them from the beginning?

Questions to Consider

When you walk into a room, do people know who you are and what you represent based on your reputation that you've established for yourself? Or do you have to tell them?

Many people today communicate via social media, texts, email, and so on. In my time, we picked up the phone and had face-to-face conversations. In today's world, how do you communicate the best and how do you communicate the worst? Why?

What kind of audience or crowd do you attract? If you're standing somewhere, do you attract people from positive backgrounds and natures or people from negative ones?

One take away from this chapter is to understand how students or coworkers see you. Perhaps give them an anonymous survey and ask them to be extremely honest. You want to get the best answers and most honest (but not necessarily positive) feedback possible.

Chapter Six: Are We for the Kids or Are We Kidding?

Living Up to Your Choice to Become an Educator

"Our job is not to prepare students for something. Our job is to help students prepare themselves for anything."
— A. J. Juliani —

It can be challenging to know which parenting and teaching strategies promote learning in the high-pressure, high-stakes school game. A successful experience in school is not only about report cards, grades, or even the goals set for a child at the beginning of the year. Ideally, children will all still learn how to learn, to retain information, to think independently, to ask questions, and to develop an increasing sense of competence.

Very young children are naturally driven to learn and explore. They are at the beginning of their lifelong quest to understand and gain mastery of the world around them. As they reach out, fall, and get back up again, they gain a heightened sense of knowledge, competence, and self-efficacy.

Somewhere around kindergarten, however, parents and teachers begin to undermine this process by devaluing the process of learning and replacing it with a mad dash for the end products. Suddenly, the intrinsic motivators of natural curiosity, competency, and self-efficacy are less valuable than extrinsic motivators, such as stickers, points, and grades. Unfortunately, these extrinsic motivators undermine kids' desire to learn over the long term.

Do you want your kids to lose interest in school? Do you wonder why your children are disengaged in the classroom and resort to choices and behaviors that go against classroom expectations?

This chapter dives deeper into one particular school motto, "Are we for the kids or are we kidding?" This came to me because, as I looked around the school where I was principal and thought about things that we were doing over the years, the question applied not only to me but to my staff.

Are we for the kids or are we kidding? Did we wake up this morning to come in and do the work that we profess to love, educate our students to help mold their future, and do what needs to be done for them?

I asked the teachers this question then told them just to think and not answer it directly. I wanted them to ponder it. For the entire year, in everything they did on a daily basis—walking into the building, walking into class, walking the halls at the end of the day, even driving home—I wanted them to ask themselves, "Was that for the kids today or was I just kidding?"

It's hard to know what to do today. A lot of children and young people use social media. They have cell phones or other devices in front of them at all times. As a child coming up in the '70s and early '80s, when we ate cereal on Saturday morning, our entertainment was the cereal box. We'd play the games or do the puzzles. I remember one particular cereal, Trix. In the commercial, the rabbit would always play silly tricks on the kids and try to take the cereal from them. Someone would pull it back and say, "Silly Rabbit, Trix are for kids."

When you think about kids, are we here for them? Or are we playing tricks or doing things that are not in compliance or within what we profess to do as educators and professionals? It again takes me back to, "Are for the kids or are we kidding?"

This is the profession we chose. We went to school to earn a degree to teach or administer in the education arena, or perhaps we came into education by default, and it was not what we originally went to school for. Either way, we still chose this option, the path of being in education.

When you made that choice, if you were honest to yourself, were you doing it for the kids? Or were you doing it for a paycheck to make a living? Is your passion really where you say it is? It should be. As with our students, if that passion and drive are not indeed focused on helping those in our care, there's potential for a not-so-pleasant outcome.

So, again I ask, are you for the kids or are you kidding?

When I look at this question, I reflect on the fact that I love my students. In my personal story, I came into education after serving in the military for 20 years as a U.S. Army logistics soldier. While in the military and stationed in Virginia, my son had a not-so-pleasant experience in his first-grade year at six years old.

In my household, our children did chores on weekends, and one thing was keeping the bathroom mirror clean. When my son used the restroom at school, he saw little water spots on the mirror, so he decided to do what he would do at home and get rid of those water spots. In his mind, he was doing something good, something positive, something he had learned from home.

It didn't work out the way it did at home because he didn't have the glass cleaner or the proper paper towels to clean it well. And then the custodian came in and witnessed my son doing this. He considered it negative and assumed he was defacing school property, so he decided to take my son to the assistant principal to report his vandalism of the mirror and smearing what he'd done.

I do understand that from the onset it may have looked to the custodian like that was what was happening, and he wanted to bring the act to the forefront because activities and actions like that made his job more challenging.

I can never absolutely say what my child will or will not do in my absence, but it threw me a bit that my son was being thought of negatively for something that I thought was not in his character.

When I had a chance to speak to the administrator, he shared the story with me, and the first question I asked was, "Did you talk to my son to identify if that was what he was doing? Or did you just go with the word of the custodian as an adult in the building and chastise my child?"

My son's consequence was to go around with the custodian to clean other mirrors in other bathrooms. The punishment was given to my child before they got a proper answer and understood what had actually taken place.

Luckily, I was part of the PTO School Improvement Council, so I had a voice in supporting my child. When I asked this of the assistant principal, he said, "Well, no, the custodian shared with me that your son did this. Because he did, and it was reported by an adult in the building, this is the consequence we gave him."

I asked the administrator to call my son to the office so we could find out whether what was said about him was true. When my son came to the office, I didn't want to speak or overwhelm him with why his dad was here and why he was in the principal's office.

I asked the assistant principal, "Would you please ask my son what he was doing in the restroom when the custodian walked in?" My son, as a six-year-old, conveyed his part of the story and said that he'd seen the water spots on the mirror in the bathroom as he was washing my hands, and at home, he had to clean the mirrors as a part of his chores to keep his bathroom clean, so he was trying to get rid of the water spots on the mirror. He easily conveyed that this was a positive action. He was trying to do a good thing, not defacing or destroying any property.

My initial thought was that this was the start of a negative or positive path for my child in his early educational career. When he shared that story, I looked at the assistant principal and said, "Do you now believe that my child was doing what the custodian said?" I didn't want to take anything away from the custodian as an adult in the building—he had a right to perceive things as he saw them—but I wanted the story to be more accurate.

My time as a soldier and this story with my son led me to become the educator that I am today. I saw that my child's voice was not being heard or respected. I wanted to get into a school to support and work with students whose voices may not be heard, appreciated, or even cared about.

I can't count how often I've listened to a child say when they got in trouble, "It doesn't matter what I say anyway. My mom's going to agree with the principal. The principal is going to say this, and my mom will approve it." And so, the child automatically felt defeated.

But I don't want children to be beaten down. When I walk into the building as a teacher, an administrator, and even in my current capacity, I'm an advocate for kids, especially those who have the quieter voices and the ones who do not get to be at the table all the time.

We make decisions about our kids, what we're going to do with them and for them, but so many times, we don't converse or consult with them. We may not be able to meet their needs or desires to do exactly what they want to do, but that does not negate giving them a voice and allowing them to say something. So again, are we for the kids or are we kidding? Do we come in and rule our classroom in school with an iron fist?

In Chapter Two, I said that I even made a change in my

school's schedule based on the thoughts, words, and advice of a student. I wanted them to know that their voice does matter to me. I listen, I hear, and, if possible, I implement. It's about building relationships with the students and helping them progress within your agenda to help them academically.

So, are you for the kids? If you are an educator, when you wake up in the morning, your feet hit the floor and you make that first-morning stretch, what does your mind answer? "Yes! Wow! I have another opportunity to make a difference and an impact!"

Or is your mindset negative in nature? "Oh, my goodness. Today, I have to go into this building and deal with these kids again." With this mindset, you start to see the faces of kids that are your troubles, and that attitude comes over you that you don't want to go to that particular class or interact with those special kids.

Instead, your mindset should be, "Yesterday may not have been the best, but today is a new day with a new opportunity to reach that kid."

So, again, are we for the kids or are we kidding? We can't joke around in this profession. These young people rely on us, they look up to us, and they expect certain things from us. The parents expect certain things from us as well. We're the ones who took all those steps to go to school, earn our degrees, and take on the task of educating young people.

So, what happens if you get to the point that you don't want to do it? Should you re-evaluate your career and your feelings about whether this is the career for you? Do you stay in it even when it's not for you? Are you being honest with yourself?

Like any job, if you go into the career you desired or

thought would be promising then realize it isn't what you thought or it isn't working out the way you wanted, you start building your resume and develop opportunities to do something more pleasing to you. You need to make yourself happy and do what you want to do and what's best for you. In doing so, you'll also be saving children from being on the receiving end of someone who does not want to be there. Our negative energy impacts our students in one way or another. They read us, our body language, our interactions, and our communication with them.

When I did my dissertation, I realized that one of the most significant transitions for students was from middle school in eighth grade to high school in ninth grade. I also realized that a lot of young black boys were being pushed aside in that transition. So, I started wondering if it was a cultural thing that just "is what it is" and happens all over the place.

Although there's no one answer for anything, I did find out that most of the disciplinary actions—even in a school district with 60–65% Caucasian students or an alternative school with 85–86% African-American students—were predominantly African-American males in the ninth grade.

I realized then that it was not just in my district. My research showed it to be the norm across the country. Then, when you looked at the prison system, there was a considerable similarity. This again brings up that not-so-positive but catchy phrase about the "school-to-prison pipeline."

In my eight years as a principal at an alternative school and a teacher in another school for three years, I worked with students in an alternative setting in which some would identify or label them as the "bad kids." No, they're not bad kids, but they are at risk of living up to that label. If we don't expose them to positive things and share with them positive ideas and the potential they have within themselves, our conversations will be negative. "Are you going to be like this?" "You're going to end up here." "You're going to end up there." "You're going to drop out."

Sometimes we label our students and say they're "at risk" solely based on a socioeconomic background and affiliation they can't control. They were born into their families. If they're in a low-income neighborhood, and they're trying to survive, they're just focusing on survival. Many of our kids join gangs as a part of that survival or for a sense of belonging because things aren't the way they need or want them to be at home.

We need to think about that. From whatever background or culture they come, these kids still walk into our classrooms. We expect them to be students for the teachers or administrators. But do they bring that to us? If they don't give that to us, what do we do then?

Are we for the kids? Are we there to look at their actions, thoughts, and minds and get to know them and try to teach them the content we have and ways around the circumstances they are living in or what they're experiencing in their lives?

If we're not waking up in the morning to be the best advocate and cheerleader for our students, we should go back to bed. Rita Pierson, in her TED Talk called "Every Kid Needs a Champion," talks about one incident in her class. She presented a 20-question test to her students. One young man missed 18 of 20 the questions, but on his paper, she put +2. When she conversed with the student, he asked her, "Did I fail the test? I missed 18." She replied, "But you got two right, and once we review the material and study and go over it again, I know you're going to do better."

That idea and the smile on the kid's face were positive. The teacher believed in him and didn't say that he got them all wrong. She said, "You got two right this time, and we will get more right the next time." This teacher implemented positivity for that student, creating a way for that student to say, "You know what, I yearn to do better, and this teacher believes in me." That is an example of someone who is for the kids.

We must have that mindset each day. In that TED talk, Pierson said that placing a –18 on the test sucks the life out of a student, but a plus gives them hope. We need to make sure our students have hope. It's something as simple as that, a negative versus a positive or correcting papers in green ink and not red. Certain things become standardized as negative or show something less than positive.

We need to speak life into our children. Proverbs 18:21 says, "Death and life are in the power of the tongue." We can speak about life with our children, or we can speak of death, which is not the physical end but negativity. What they hear and sense from adults regularly matters.

On my local radio station here in Columbia, South Carolina, the DJ signs off each day around two o'clock, and he says, "Parents, watch your children because they are truly watching you." That is such a true statement because the actions in our house are their reality. The steps in our classrooms are reality for them as well, so we must continue to watch our students and the oppositions and challenges they may have.

Teachers may say, "I'm not the parent. I'm not this; I'm not that." I beg to differ. That may not be what you signed up for, but anyone in this profession who has been educated realizes that we are more than teachers. We are more than administrators. We may end up being mom and dad to some, and to others a big brother, big sister, uncle, aunt, or counselor.

We are a lot of different people, and we don't wear just one hat in education. We need to give these kids what they need the most because when they're successful, we're successful. We can't play with it, and we have to be honest about it.

Based on my experiences as a principal and a teacher at an alternative school, I know I touched lives. I know I changed lives. I had one 15-year-old student who met me at a student retreat facilitated by the school, but otherwise we had never met. After the retreat, I was standing in the hallway, meeting and greeting the students coming into my class or going to other classes down the hall when this young man walked up to me and asked me if I would be his mentor. I did not even know his name at the time, but he knew my name, and who I was, because other students had talked about me.

My response to his request went a little something like this. "You have never been in any of my classes, but you know one of my students. I will be glad to help you as best I can." After making a commitment to help this young man, I relayed to him that I needed to speak with his mother because I never take on any task or responsibility regarding children without the consent of the parent or guardian.

One day, I knew this student's mother was picking him up from school, and I informed him that I would like to meet his mother. I walked out, met her, and told her about the conversation we had had. She happily agreed to provide her consent for me to begin mentoring her son. She expressed her excitement by telling me that her son needed some positive support in his life. He had dropped out of school at one point, and he had been in the gangs.

So, I mentored him. At one point, I would pick him up and take him to different places even when he had a girlfriend but didn't have a car. I would pick him up, go pick her up, drop them off at the movies, and I would go on my way and have him call me when he was done. Even outside the building, I was there for that kid because I saw potential in him.

When he dropped out of school, I told him that I don't hang out with dropouts, so I encouraged him to get back into high school. He graduated and did so on time. I also helped him enroll in a local college. He went and finished college on track in four and a half years, got his degree, and got a music career.

This young man is now 31 years old (so, it's been 16 years) and now living in Tennessee, working full time, and doing exceptionally well for himself. I'm incredibly proud of him. I put myself aside and focused on that kid. He is now also a father, and he asked me to be his child's godfather. He's doing what he needs to do, taking care of his child.

When that same young man was leaving the alternative school, getting ready to return to his home school, but he didn't want to return to it because he knew he would be faced with the same teachers and friends who got him kicked out. At that time, I was the principal of a charter school. He called and asked if he could come to my school.

Like every other student, I interviewed him and his parent to see about the potential. He was a good fit for the school, so I accepted him. This young man and I connected so quickly because of the possibility I saw in him. He did not drop out of school, and I got him into my school, and he graduated high school a year earlier than planned.

Final Thoughts

Stories like that were powerful to me, and I have many others that are similar that I could share. It was my way of saying, "I'm for that kid."

The key takeaway is for you to better understand the importance of striving to be the best fit in your position of choice by being honest with yourself and evaluating your effectiveness. When you work in a career that you do not like or does not fit you, you stand a chance of being unhappy and potentially causing others to be unhappy.

Questions to Consider

Why did you choose education as your profession?

Is this your career or passion or simply just a job?

How do you identify the potential in a student or a peer and convey it to them?

What do you like the most and least about your career choice?

How often do you reflect on your influence and react to that reflection?

Chapter Seven: Focus 20/20 Vision

Viewing Life Like a Camera (If it Isn't Clear, Make the Adjustment and Refocus.)

"Prioritizing sharpens your vision so you can focus on the most important things."
— Myles Munroe —

As you reflect and think about everything covered throughout the different chapters of this book, what is your vision for your students? Do you plan on implementing new techniques and strategies within your classroom or even in your life? Or are you going to continue to do what you have been doing and expect different results?

If you've made it this far, I expect that you will continue to push the needle forward in the classroom and bridge the gap between where education currently is and where you want it to be. Spend some time reflecting and looking back over the previous chapters after doing your self-evaluations then look at your students, put things into practice, ask yourself the questions, and implement some of the recommended suggestions.

How is the picture looking for you now? Is it clear? Is it a little bit more apparent than it was? Or is it still very distorted or unclear?

When thinking about 20/20 vision, I remember when I retired from the U.S. Army in 2005. I was almost 38 years old, and the doctor told me during my exit physical, "You may want to take another look at your eyes when you hit 40." He was saying that even though I'd never needed glasses and had great vision as a child and throughout my entire military career, over time our vision changes. Our sight is not always what it was.

That was eye-opening for a person who had never worn glasses, but I know people who have worn glasses all their life. For example, my wife has been wearing glasses since elementary school, and so her conception of things was already challenged then with the potential of getting better or worse through the years.

Today, we have so much technology and procedures to

correct our sight, but when one sense is minimized, another becomes keener. Think about some famous people, such as Stevie Wonder and Ray Charles, who had challenges with sight and yet lived successful, prosperous lives. Did their challenge stop them from doing and being what they wanted? Of course, they had limitations, and some things were missed in their lives, but they also had many successes and achievements that some of us, with full sight, will never do or accomplish.

That perspective emphasizes that your focus either can always be within the immediate scope of your eyes, or you can choose to focus beyond your current activity, purpose, and direction.

Think about being a teacher and waking up in the morning. What is your expectation of yourself first and foremost? Then how does that bleed over into or lend itself to the expectations you have around students? Are you focused? If you're not focused, how can you help your students focus?

I recently posted a meme that got a lot of feedback from my family and friends. It was a picture of a young man in profile with the caption, "I don't need medicine to help me focus. I need someone focused on helping me." That blew my mind. As an educator, I can't tell you how often I've sat in meetings with students and families with the purpose of identifying or labeling a child with ADD or ADHD, meaning that the child has a problem focusing and is easily distracted into doing other things.

Thinking back to when I was an adult in my graduate and doctoral programs, many times I took classes on Saturdays. During the course, I really missed watching college football. We all were required to have a laptop and our books in class with us. The professors stood at the front of the class, and I was in the class with my computer open, but many times I had a minimized screen of the football game so I could see how my favorite team was faring in the game. Was I as focused as I needed to be at all times during my doctoral program? Not at all.

I also have witnessed this with my teachers and staff when I served as a principal. I would stand up in front of the team ready to present our professional development, and I would sometimes see my teachers on their cell phones or talking to each other or having sidebar conversations. Did I have their undivided attention? Not always.

In the classroom as a teacher, we create the best lesson plans to present content to our students, and then we get somewhat defeated when we stand before the class and have to stop the class frequently to ask a student to settle down and be quiet and then regain control the conversation.

In a nutshell, our attention span as a species is not the greatest. Many times, our attention is diverted by the things around us. As I dictated and wrote this book, I sat in a room by myself away from any distractions. There was no music in the background. There was no television nor anything else to distract me because I know myself. I know I can be easily distracted and taken away from the purpose of what I've set down to do. Thankfully, as an adult I was able to reel myself back in to focus and successfully finish my doctoral program, my dissertation, and more.

Even with this book, I give so much credit to Kyle S. King, my book coach, an outstanding young man with so much patience and potential for helping people such as myself. I remember telling him not so long ago that I thought my delay in finishing the book was because I was lazy. He didn't like the term lazy, and he shared that with me.

Even though I was calling myself lazy, I had to think about what he said to me. He said that a lazy person could not have been a successful school leader. A lazy person could not have had a successful 20-year career in the military. A lazy person could not finish a dissertation in two years. All the things he knew about me informed him that I was not being lazy. Although I may have changed my focus on things at times, I was able to refocus.

I remember a song by Johnny Nash that says, "I can see clearly now the rain is gone. I can see all obstacles in my way." Those few words remind me that we are going to have barriers. There will be cloudy days or days that may not be as productive as we want them to be. But we can refocus. We can get back on track and get our vision back.

Your vision does not necessarily mean having 20/20 vision as you focus on what is purposeful, right, and ringing true in your life. Perfect vision is called 20/20, and if your eyes do not provide you with that perfect vision, an optometrist will offer or suggest corrective lenses to help you reach that ideal. Do you have corrective lenses? If so, are they clear? Or do you need to pay another visit to the optometrist to regain your focus?

Again, our vision changes through the years, so you need to check your eyes then go back every year or two. I now wear glasses because I need them for reading. I also recently have been diagnosed as potentially having glaucoma, which limits my peripheral vision. It can't be corrected, but with medication and treatment, I can keep it from becoming worse. Changes like these may cause us to need an adjustment in our lenses. Each time you get checked, your vision may be the same or you may have lost a little or have other things that impact your physical ability of seeing.

In that light, how do we keep our focus on our students, our job, and our career to keep them from getting worse? We may not be able to go back and fix things we did wrong—perhaps how we spoke to students or made decisions in the past—but we can stop it from getting worse by refocusing.

That is the key, and it doesn't mean I need medicine to help me focus. I need someone focused on helping me. As instructors, we should be that very person who is focused on helping our students. If we're not focused on helping them, our vision, their vision, and the idea of their future can be bleak. We need to keep striving for 20/20 vision and refocus when it lacks.

When we look at things—a situation or a student—on the surface, do we see them how they are presented? Or do we need to peel back the layers of the onion to say, "I know this kid. Of course, I see the physical body of this kid, but is this kid truly who I see before me?"

We all have layers, but sometimes we don't like people to peel back layers because we like our privacy. It's the same with our students. Some of our students are not as open to wanting us to peel back their layers. But building a relationship with them and trying to understand their potential then conveying the potential we see in them could allow them to say, "I trust you. I believe in you because you believe in me."

Your focus on that kid is still professional, but now that kid knows you care about them. You have focused on them. You have built a relationship with them. In the absence of that focus, we're just going through the motions every day hoping things will work out. Instead, we must be purposeful and mindful of the focus we have on our students and their future.

In truth, our goal is not just to get the students across the stage at the end of 12th grade but to give them a mindset of wanting to have something outside of school as young adults, as contributing citizens in our community. We want them to give back to those who have provided for them. Those are the things I consider when I think about focus.

I pride myself on seeing the potential in people that others may not. I once had a student who had spent 18 months in the Department of Juvenile Justice. The charter school rules and admission process stated that if a student came to me from such a placement of dealing with behaviors or criminal acts, they needed to go to an alternative setting.

At this point, as principal of a charter school and not an alternative school, I typically would not enroll a kid like that, but there was something about him that I saw in our conversations when I interviewed him and his mother. There was something about the things he said, his actions, his behaviors, his demeanor, and his mother's support of him that just pulled me and pulled me. It was almost like I'd had a lens that was very blurry with what I first saw of his story—the trouble, the issues, and concerns—but as I sat there listening to them, my lens started to focus on myself more than on them.

I saw that this student could and would do good things. I took a risk and accepted him into my school. He was a year and a half behind his graduation year, a lot of which came from the outside activities that had caused him to be incarcerated in the juvenile detention center. Still, I saw the potential of him buying into my school. I pushed him and pushed him and built a relationship with him. I spoke with his mother and realized two months later that she attended my church. We went at different times, but I went an extra time one day to see them.

Seeing them in the church gave me another connection to this young man's potential. Despite his life challenges, he still came to church with his mother at 17 years old. He might have done the things that had caused him to go to juvie, but he still had respect for his mother and honored her requirement for him to be in church with her.

Building those relationships is how we focus. When we focus on our students, we always can adjust and change that focus. We may not initially see the whole person or the path to help them at the onset, but we can always refocus.

I know that the first impression is important, but if we think about refocusing to get that 20/20 vision, we may learn that what we initially saw was not accurate. We can't take that first impression away from ourselves or anyone else, but as we get to know a person, the actual person, can that change our vision and what we see or think about them? I say yes.

We all can improve our focus. You could be someone who never had to wear glasses or corrective lenses, but that doesn't mean you don't still need to focus. It is not always the physical sight or a lack of presence. It could still be focusing on issues, things, and considerations about a person.

As educators, our students will show us who their parents are when they get dropped off or taken to the bus stop. These parents are not sending us just whatever is in the house, they are sending us the best they have: their child. Even if there was some difficulty in the kid's upbringing, a collaborative effort with those parents will show that I have that child's best interest at heart.

I see things that parents may not see. I've had to call home, and the parents say, "Well, they don't do that at home." As I addressed earlier, my work me and my home me can be different. Do I want to be the same person in all venues? Maybe I do. Maybe I don't. We all deserve to let our hair down, be who we are, and do what we feel like we want to do, but there's a cost and a consequence at times for those things, so we need to stay focused on what's real.

I've heard people say that sometimes we "major on a minor," meaning that an infraction can be something very minute or minimal that doesn't really warrant a disciplinary action or punishment, but we focus on it so much that we lose sight of the real concern.

An alternative school often is a student's last stop before being expelled and sitting at home on the couch for the school year. If they can't make it in an alternative school, the only other resort is to go home. But I can't reach a child from their couch. I need them in the building.

I spent my first year as principal of the alternative school getting to know the students as they got to know me. I recommended 89 students for expulsion in my first year at that school. That 89 dropped to 13 and 12 students in Years 2 and 3, respectively, because I realized I had to be more creative in my consequences to reach the students. Putting them out of school and suspending them was giving a three-day vacation to kids who didn't want to be in school anyway. If they said a particular word, I gave a specific action. If what they did wasn't criminal or highly disruptive, I would find a consequence to support them that made sense.

I focused on ensuring that my values came through in the consequences for infractions. In the military, if you missed formation, you had to focus on your time management to be at a particular place at a specific time. Something like making me cut the grass would have had nothing to do with my being late, so that punishment did not fit the infraction.

In the military, we had a term called "school the soldier." If being on time was a concern, you would go through a series of activities related to time. Because you missed time in formation, on a Saturday (when you would typically have free time) you were required to report to the unit's 24-hour surveillance front desk in a different uniform every hour. It wasn't possible to go back to your room, take a nap, wake up, and return because you had to be in a different uniform every time you came downstairs. This was a way of making sure that the soldier could see how their consequence related to their infraction.

This also goes back to the story of the student who decided to take the school's American flag. In his discipline, it was my duty to make sure the student learned a valuable lesson that was reasonable and related to the infraction.

Final Thoughts

As you reflect on this chapter, I want you to think about one of life's most precious gifts: the gift of sight. In this context, sight refers to vision; however, we know that vision and sight can be very different when you consider the two terms together.

For example, Helen Keller, who was blind and deaf, once said, "The only thing worse than being blind is having sight but no vision." She went on to have a successful life despite the absence of sight and hearing, which we often take for granted. I think she was able to be positive and successful despite her situation from something else she said:

"The best and most beautiful things in the world cannot be seen or even touched—they must be felt with the heart."

It has been said that educators do not enter this profession to become rich; we enter this profession because of our love of education and helping children. As I posed in Chapter 6, "Are we for the kids or are we kidding?" I would love to think that those of us who chose this career path did so because of our vision and desire to support and help prepare those who will lead us and care for us in the future.

People may or may not be aware that Walt Disney died four years before the famed amusement park even opened. Some said that it was a shame he did not get to see his dream come true. But the truth is that he saw it all before any of us ever had the chance to enjoy it. After all, he was the brainchild behind that amazing attraction we all now enjoy today.

Educators, this is you! And, to do that, we need to focus on our students. If we don't, who will? If we're not there, who will be there for them?

Questions to Consider

Can you see success in yourself, in your students, or in your coworkers now or in the future?

In your years in education, how has your focus on your career changed?

How has your view of education and students changed from when you were a student to getting your education to being an educator today?

How do you regain your focus once it has become blurred? Do you refocus your lens or do you need a new one?

Identify your strengths and any weaknesses that you'd like to improve. Document those adjustments over time (a week or a month).

Write down your 5- to 10-year plan as a letter to your future self. Then reach for the goals that focus on your future.

Every week, positively encourage a student about their future and their potential. Speaking life into our students allows them to be successful.

Conclusion

"Children are human beings to whom respect is due, superior to us by reason of their innocence and of the greater possibilities of their future."
— Maria Montessori —

It is my desire that educators will take the opportunity to see the whole child and not prematurely label them with a title that may end up governing their lives.

We all deserve the opportunity to be the best people we can be. Often, that takes support, guidance, and direction from the adults that these kids meet in their lives. As educators, we cannot afford to be negative influences. Today's students are the doctors, lawyers, and leaders of tomorrow. It's our job to show them that those credentials are within reach for every one of them.

I hope that, as you have read this book and examined the individual chapters by both title and content, you will be able to continue the great work you already do as educators and create a culture of inclusion as we develop these young minds.

Think of the students you teach as sponges ready to soak up the knowledge you have. Encourage them to take your knowledge and make it theirs. It is through our profession as educators that all other professions are possible. We spearhead a society of people who will take what we have shared with them into the world.

Also remember that you are not in this alone. We have access to other highly effective educators and administrators in our buildings. Build that network of professionals to help you grow your skillset. In return, give back what you learn to someone else. It is with this process that we continue to improve upon the best and most needed profession.

Take the time to take care of yourself while taking care of others. Education is always changing, and self-care is extremely important. One of the worst things we can do is be present but not have our presence felt. Our students know if we are in it for them or in it for the paycheck.

We owe it to them to be in it for them. Those relationships are important and necessary. We may not always consider our interactions with students or colleagues as relationships. But, in all honesty, they are real and ongoing relationships. When two or more people come together—even for a short period of time—we are, in fact, establishing a relationship of some sort. In this case it is professional.

Rita Pierson also said in her Ted Talk that "students don't learn from people they don't like." We may not be looking to be friends with our students, but the relationship of trust and care that you build with them is based on your heart, and your love for education will be evident to them.

Allow me to conclude by saying thank you for what you do as educators. You are needed and appreciated. Some days may be tougher than others, and some relationships may be tougher than others, but it is worth it in the end.

Our students need us now, just as we will need them in the future. What we are doing is investing in their future as well as our own. Once we remove the labels and get to know them, we can reach them and then teach them.

RESOURCES AND REFERENCES

Ballard, G., & Garret, S. (1988). "Man in the Mirror" [Recorded by M. Jackson]. *Bad.* Epic Records: New York, NY.

Covey, S. M. R. (2006). *Speed of trust: The one thing that changes everything.* Simon & Schuster. New York, NY.

Elias, M. (2013). The school-to-prison pipeline: Policies and practices that favor incarceration over education do us all a grave injustice. *Learning for Justice, 43.* Retrieved at https://www.learningforjustice.org/magazine/spring-2013/the-school-to-prison-pipeline

Maxwell, J. C. (2011). *The 360-degree leader: Developing your influence from anywhere in the organization.* HarperCollins Leadership: Nashville, TN.

Mills, P. D. (2019). *Evaluation of alternative schools in South Carolina: A companion dissertation.* Publication No. #ED565554) [Ed.D., Gardner-Webb University]. ERIC. https://eric.ed.gov/?id=ED565554

Nash, J. (1972). "I Can See Clearly Now." *I Can See Clearly Now.* Epic Records: New York, NY.

Pierson, R. (May 3, 2013). *Every kid needs a champion* [Video]. Ted Conferences. https://www.ted.com/talks/rita_pierson_every_kid_needs_a_champion?language=en

Seuss, Dr. (1957). *How the grinch stole Christmas!* Random House: New York, NY.

Whitaker, T. (2014). *Shifting the monkey: The art of protecting good people from liars, criers, and other slackers.* Solution Tree: Bloomington, IN.

ACKNOWLEDGMENTS

Now that I have taken the time to sit down and complete this book, I want to give special thanks to everyone responsible for pushing me toward fulfilling not only to achieve this dream but also, through my experiences, give a part of myself to prayerfully support teachers and staff and, most importantly, the students.

Thanks to my wife (Sharon R. Ham-Mills), who often would tell me to find a quiet place and get busy writing my book. She saw and heard my dream for years and knew my passion for my work better than anyone. The love, the push, and the partnership we have shared for the past three decades do not go unappreciated.

Thanks to my mom in Heaven (Lillie M. Jones-Mills), who I know is continuing to look down on me from above as a beacon of light and encouragement. Mom, I will continue to do my best to make you proud, and I miss you here daily!

To my adult children, Keyasha and Perry, Jr., thank you for being my cheerleaders and being those extra voices of encouragement for me to follow through with my dream. I am proud of both of you and love you both dearly.

Lastly, to my writing coach Kyle S. King, thank you for being available and willing to hold me accountable for what you believed I could do and pushing me to tell *my* story as only I could.

ABOUT THE AUTHOR

Dr. Perry D. Mills, Sr., is a native of Darlington, South Carolina. He is an only child and was raised by a single mother. He attended Darlington County Public Schools, from which he graduated in 1985.

As a young person, Dr. Mills had a dislike for school, which led to his early enlistment upon graduation (at age 17) into the U.S. Army where he served proudly for 20 years—living abroad in Korea, Germany, and Italy as well as domestically—until his retirement in 2005.

After basic training, his first assignment in Korea left him living far from family and friends and looking for a hobby. His interest in photos and a new camera led him to take his first college course in photography. That one class taken as an adult ignited his newfound passion for learning and education. During his time in the military, Dr. Mills went on to earn an associate degree in Liberal Arts, a bachelor's degree in Human Resources Administration, and master's degrees in Human Resources Management and Human Resources Development.

Dr. Mills also served six months in Iraq during Desert Shield Desert Storm in 1991, and his stateside assignments included Fort Sill, Oklahoma; Fort Monroe, Virginia; Fort Lee, Virginia; and Fort Jackson, South Carolina, from which he retired in August 2005.

Upon his retirement, Dr. Mills joined the Troops to Teachers Program and began his education career in the classroom teaching high school business education at the Olympia Learning Center in Columbia, South Carolina. Dr. Mills was named his school's Teacher of the Year in 2007.

In his second year in the classroom, he decided he wanted to make a greater impact in leadership and began pursuing his Education Specialist Degree (Ed. S) in Education Leadership.

Near the end of his third classroom year, he began pursuing school leadership opportunities and was promoted to assistant principal at Polo Road Elementary School, for his fourth year in education. About midway through that year, Mills was approached and encouraged to apply for a newly opened position as the principal of the alternative school in the district. In 2009, he applied and was promoted to principal of Blythewood Academy, where he served until June 2017.

In July 2017, he was offered another challenging opportunity, to serve as the principal for the Richland Two Charter High School in Columbia. He served there through February 2021. Dr. Mills then moved on to serve as the Director of Federal Programs for the Sumter School District in Sumter, South Carolina. Currently he serves as the Chief Program Officer for the South Carolina Public Charter School District.

After his own children graduated from high school, Dr. Mills decided to return to the classroom in August 2011 to pursue his doctorate degree in Education Administration and Leadership and completed the program in August 2013. His dissertation is titled *A Program Evaluation of Alternative Schools in North and South Carolina: A Companion Dissertation.*

As an educator, he has participated in several educational seminars, workshops, and other professional development opportunities, including the South Carolina Principal Induction Program and the South Carolina School Leadership Executive Institute. He also has served as a South Carolina Education Policy Fellow.

Dr. Mills resides in Blythewood, South Carolina, with his wife Sharon of more than 35 years. They have two adult children, Keyasha and Perry, Jr.

CONNECT WITH THE AUTHOR

Thank you for reading
Unknown Labels: Know Me Before You Label Me.

Dr. Mills can't wait to connect with you! Here are a few ways you can contact the author:

- **LinkedIn:** http://www.linkedin.com/in/dr-perry-d-mills-sr-71233b51
- **Facebook:** https://www.facebook.com/perry.millssr
- **Email:** perrydmills@outlook.com

www.ingramcontent.com/pod-product-compliance
Lightning Source LLC
Chambersburg PA
CBHW031212270326
41931CB00006B/533

* 9 7 9 8 2 1 8 2 5 4 6 1 2 *